Bank Reconciliation Essentials

Steven M. Bragg

Table of Contents

About the Author

Steven Bragg, CPA, has been the chief financial officer or controller of four companies, as well as a consulting manager at Ernst & Young. He received a master's degree in finance from Bentley College, an MBA from Babson College, and a Bachelor's degree in Economics from the University of Maine. He has been a two-time president of the Colorado Mountain Club, and is an avid alpine skier, mountain biker, and certified master diver. Mr. Bragg resides in Centennial, Colorado. He has written more than 300 books and courses, including *New Controller Guidebook*, *GAAP Guidebook*, and *Payroll Management*.

Steven maintains the accountingtools.com web site, which contains continuing professional education courses, the Accounting Best Practices podcast, and thousands of articles on accounting subjects.

Buy Additional AccountingTools Courses

AccountingTools offers more than 1,500 hours of CPE courses, with concentrations in accounting, auditing, finance, taxation, and ethics. Related courses that you might like include:

- Accountants' Guidebook
- Bookkeeping Guidebook
- Closing the Books

Go to accountingtools.com/cpe to view these additional courses.

Bank Reconciliation Essentials

Introduction

A bank reconciliation is an essential component of the monthly closing process. It is used to ensure that the cash records of an organization's bank match its own internal records. Without this periodic cross-check, it is quite likely that the entity will eventually have a cash figure on its books that departs noticeably from reality. In this manual, we discuss the purpose of a bank reconciliation, how to conduct it, and the nature of the various issues that are likely to be found during a typical reconciliation process.

The Purpose of a Bank Reconciliation

A bank reconciliation is used to compare your records to those of your bank, to see if there are any differences between these two sets of records for your cash transactions. The ending balance of your version of the cash records is known as the book balance, while the bank's version is called the bank balance. It is extremely common for there to be differences between the two balances, which you should track down and adjust in your own records. If you were to ignore these differences, there would eventually be substantial variances between the amount of cash that you think you have and the amount the bank says that you actually have in an account. The result could be an overdrawn bank account, bounced checks, and overdraft fees. In some cases, the bank may even elect to shut down your bank account.

It is also useful to complete a bank reconciliation to see if any customer checks have bounced, or if any checks you issued were altered or even stolen and cashed without your knowledge. Thus, fraud detection is a key reason for completing a bank reconciliation. When there is an ongoing search for fraudulent transactions, it may be necessary to reconcile a bank account on a daily basis, in order to obtain early warning of a problem.

When it comes time for the annual audit, the auditors will always examine the company's ending bank reconciliation as part of their testing procedures, so this is yet another reason to complete a reconciliation.

The Bank Statement

A bank statement is a document that is issued by a bank once a month to its clients, listing the transactions impacting a bank account. The statement provides the following information:

+	The beginning cash balance in the account
+	The total amount of each deposited batch of checks and cash
-	Funds withdrawn from the account
-	Individual checks paid
+	Interest earned on the account
-	Service fees and penalties charged against the account
=	Ending cash balance in the account

The bank statement shows the cumulative balance of cash in the account, net of all the preceding transactions, as of the end of each day in the reporting period. Some banks still print these statements along with an accompanying set of images of all cleared checks.

Bank statements do not necessarily mirror the days in a calendar month. Instead, customers may request that their bank statements cover a one-month period that ends on a different date (for example, the 25th day of the month).

Reasons Why the Bank Balance Differs from the Book Balance

The bank balance reported by your bank is usually different from the book balance in your accounting records. There are several reasons for this difference, which are as follows:

- *Outstanding checks*. The company has issued checks that have not yet been presented to the bank for payment. Since they have not been presented, the bank does not record these checks in its records. This difference will eventually vanish, when the bank receives the checks.
- *Deposits in transit*. The company records received cash and then sends the cash to the bank. If the cash is still in transit as of month-end, then the bank will not record it until the following month. As was the case with outstanding checks, this difference will vanish when the bank receives the deposits.
- *Interest on deposited cash*. Depending on the nature of the bank account, the bank may credit interest income to the account. The company is not aware of this amount until the bank statement arrives, and so has not yet recorded it.
- *Bank service fees*. The bank charges the account for a variety of services, and removes the related cash from the company's account. The company is not aware of these charges until the bank statement arrives, and so has not yet recorded them.

- *Check printing charges.* The bank charges the company to print additional checks for it, and removes the related cash from the company's account. The company is not aware of the amount of this charge until the bank statement arrives, and so has not yet recorded it.
- *Bank error.* The bank has incorrectly recorded a transaction. In this case, the bank must be notified to correct the error.
- *Company error.* The company has incorrectly recorded a cash-related transaction. In this case, the company accountant corrects the error.

When any of these differences have already been recorded in the company's records but not those of the bank, they are itemized as reconciling items on the bank reconciliation. Examples are outstanding checks and deposits in transit. Outstanding checks are listed as a deduction from the bank balance, while deposits in transit are added to the bank balance.

Some of these differences will need to be recorded on the books of the company; using journal entries. Examples of items to be recorded in this manner are the interest on deposited cash, bank service fees, check printing charges, and company recordation errors.

The Bank Reconciliation

It is extremely important to complete a bank reconciliation for every account that contains a significant amount of cash. This is needed to obtain an understanding of the types and timing of cash flows and the unrecorded transactions that can arise, as well as to ensure that the company's cash balance information is correct.

A likely outcome of the reconciliation process will be several adjustments to a company's recorded cash balance. It is unlikely that a company's ending cash balance and the bank's ending cash balance will be identical, since there are probably multiple payments and deposits in transit at all times, as well as bank service fees, penalties, and not sufficient funds deposits that the company has not yet recorded.

The essential process flow for a bank reconciliation is to start with the bank's ending cash balance (known as the *bank balance*), add to it any deposits in transit from the company to the bank, subtract any checks that have not yet cleared the bank, and either add or deduct any other reconciling items. Then find the company's ending cash balance and deduct from it any bank service fees, not sufficient funds (NSF) checks and penalties, and add to it any interest earned. At the end of this process, the adjusted bank balance should equal the company's ending adjusted cash balance.

The following bank reconciliation procedure assumes that the bank reconciliation is being created in an accounting software package, which makes the reconciliation process easier:

1. Enter the bank reconciliation software module. A listing of uncleared checks and uncleared deposits will appear.
2. Go to the checks section of the bank reconciliation module. The system will display a list of uncleared checks. Match this list of checks against the list of checks that have cleared the bank, as listed on the bank statement. Check off

in the bank reconciliation module all checks that are listed on the bank statement as having cleared the bank. The following issues may arise:

- If any checks recorded by the bank as having cleared are listed on the bank statement with different amounts than what the company recorded, access the check image posted on the bank's website to verify the amount on the check. If the company recorded it incorrectly, make an adjusting entry to match the amount of the check to the amount recorded by the bank.
- If any checks recorded by the bank as having cleared are listed incorrectly by the bank, contact the bank and send them documentation of the error. This difference between the recorded amounts of the bank and the company will remain until such time as the bank adjusts its recorded amount. In the meantime, the difference will be a reconciling item.

3. Check off in the bank reconciliation module all deposits that are listed on the bank statement as having cleared the bank. The following issues may arise:

- The bank may have recorded some deposits that the company did not record. If so, access the check image posted on the bank's website to verify who issued the check and the amount of it. Record this deposit in the company's records.
- The company may have recorded some deposits that were not recorded by the bank. This may be due to a not sufficient funds situation, or because the bank does not accept foreign checks. These deposits will be reconciling items until such time as the company can convince the bank to deposit them or finds an alternative way to convert the deposited checks to cash. It may also require the reversal of these deposited items in the records of the company.

4. Enter as expenses all bank charges appearing on the bank statement, and which have not already been recorded in the company's records. Examples of these charges are not sufficient funds fees, check printing fees, and bank service fees (such as for check processing, direct deposit payments, and wire transfer fees).

5. Enter the ending balance on the bank statement. If the book and bank balances match, then post all changes recorded in the bank reconciliation, and close the module. If the balances do *not* match, then continue reviewing the bank reconciliation for additional reconciling items. Look for the following items:

- Checks recorded in the bank records at a different amount from what is recorded in the company's records.
- Deposits recorded in the bank records at a different amount from what is recorded in the company's records.

- Checks recorded in the bank records that are not recorded at all in the company's records.
- Deposits recorded in the bank records that are not recorded at all in the company's records.
- Inbound wire transfers from which a processing fee has been extracted.

6. Continue the investigation. If there is an undocumented reconciling item, review the bank reconciliation process steps just noted. If there is still an undocumented variance, go back to the bank reconciliations for the preceding periods and see if the variance arose in a prior period.
7. If the remaining difference is immaterial, it may be acceptable to record the difference in the company's books, rather than spending time on additional investigation activities.

EXAMPLE

Suture Corporation is closing its books for the month ended April 30. Suture's accountant must prepare a bank reconciliation based on the following issues:

1. The bank statement contains an ending bank balance of $320,000.
2. The bank statement contains a $200 check printing charge for new checks that the company ordered.
3. The bank statement contains a $150 service charge for operating the bank account.
4. The bank rejected a deposit of $500 due to not sufficient funds, and charges the company a $10 fee associated with the rejection.
5. The bank statement contains interest income of $30.
6. Suture issued $80,000 of checks that have not yet cleared the bank.
7. Suture deposited $25,000 of checks at month-end that were not deposited in time to appear on the bank statement.

The accountant creates the following reconciliation:

		Item #	Adjustment to Books
Bank balance	$320,000	1	
- Check printing charge	-200	2	Debit expense, credit cash
- Service charge	-150	3	Debit expense, credit cash
- NSF fee	-10	4	Debit expense, credit cash
- NSF deposit rejected	-500	4	Debit receivable, credit cash
+ Interest income	+30	5	Debit cash, credit interest income
- Uncleared checks	-80,000	6	None
+ Deposits in transit	+25,000	7	None
= Book balance	$264,170		

When the bank reconciliation process is complete, print a report through the accounting software that shows the bank and book balances, the identified differences between the two (most likely to be uncleared checks), and any remaining unreconciled difference. Retain a copy of this report for each month, since the outside auditors will want to see them as part of the year-end audit.

The format of the report will vary by software package; a simplistic layout follows.

Sample Bank Reconciliation Statement

For the month ended March 31, 20x3		
Bank balance	$850,000	
Less: Checks outstanding	-225,000	See detail
Add: Deposits in transit	+100,000	See detail
+/- Other adjustments	0	
Book balance	$725,000	
Unreconciled difference	$0	

The standard approach to bank reconciliations is to complete them for all accounts shortly after the end of each month, since the reconciliations are derived from the bank statements that are issued after month-end.

> **Note:** Many banks include a blank bank reconciliation statement in their month-end account statements, for the use of account holders. Providing this form is also useful for the bank, since it encourages account holders to attend to the transactions flowing through their accounts, and so clears up any long-term confusion about account balances.

If there is so little activity in a bank account that there really is no need for a periodic bank reconciliation, you should question why the account even exists. It may be better to terminate the account and roll any residual funds into a more active account. By doing so, it may be easier to invest the residual funds, as well as to monitor the status of the investment.

Problems with Bank Reconciliations

There are several problems that continually arise as part of the bank reconciliation, and which you should be aware of. They are as follows:

- *Uncleared checks that continue to not be presented.* There will be a residual number of checks that either are not presented to the bank for payment for a long time, or which are never presented for payment. In the short term, you should treat them in the same manner as any other uncleared checks – just keep them in the uncleared checks listing in your accounting software, so they will be an ongoing reconciling item. In the long term, you should contact the payee to see if they ever received the check; you will likely need to void the old check and issue them a new one.

- *Checks clear the bank after having been voided.* As noted in the preceding special issue, if a check remains uncleared for a long time, you will probably void the old check and issue a replacement check. But what if the payee then cashes the original check? If you voided it with the bank, the bank should reject the check when it is presented. If you did not void it with the bank, then you must record the check with a credit to the cash account and a debit to indicate the reason for the payment (such as an expense account, or an increase in a cash account or decrease in a liability account). If the payee has not yet cashed the replacement check, you should void it with the bank at once, to avoid a double payment. Otherwise, you will need to pursue repayment of the second check with the payee.
- *Deposited checks are returned.* There are cases where the bank will refuse to deposit a check, usually because it is drawn on a bank account located in another country. In this case, you must reverse the original entry related to that deposit, which will be a credit to the cash account to reduce the cash balance, with a corresponding debit (increase) in the accounts receivable account.

Another possibility that may be causing problems is that the dates covered by the bank statement have changed so that some items are included or excluded. This situation should only arise if someone at the company requested the bank to alter the closing date for the company's bank account.

Bank Reconciliation Record Keeping

Bank reconciliation statements should be retained and archived by period, so that they are readily accessible when needed during the annual audit. The auditors will want to verify the preparation of this statement for at least the year-end bank reconciliation. In addition, if the auditors have chosen to engage in interim audit procedures, they may elect to review the most recent reconciliation as of that date.

Bank Reconciliation Concepts

There are a number of concepts that you will encounter while conducting a bank reconciliation. In the following sub-sections, we discuss the nature of each one. They are listed in alphabetical order.

Bank Charges

A bank charge is a fee assessed against an account by a financial institution. A bank charge may be levied for a number of reasons, including the following:

- Not maintaining a minimum balance
- Issuing a not sufficient funds check
- Depositing a check that bounces

- Exceeding the overdraft on the account
- The passage of time, if there is a monthly service fee
- The ordering of additional bank checks
- Foreign transaction fees
- The issuance of a paper bank statement, rather than an on-line one
- The manual handling of transactions by a bank teller
- Inactivity in an account

A business that incurs bank charges will usually record them as expenses as part of its monthly bank reconciliation process.

Bank Debits

Bank debits are transactions that reduce the balance in a customer's account at a bank. Larger debits are usually associated with checks written by a bank customer to a payee, or withdrawals directly made by a customer from their own account. Smaller debits can be associated with the imposition of bank fees, such as for check printing, check processing, deposit processing, foreign transactions, minimum balances, monthly maintenance, not sufficient funds checks, and for the delivery of a paper statement.

Bank Errors

Bank errors are transactions that have been incorrectly recorded by a bank in a customer's account. These errors are usually found during the monthly bank reconciliation process conducted by the bank's customers, who notify the bank to correct the indicated items. There are usually few bank errors, which are concentrated in the areas of incorrect check and deposit amounts. It is also possible that a bank will debit an account for services that were not actually provided to the customer.

Cancelled Checks

A cancelled check is a check payment for which the stated amount of cash has been removed from the payer's checking account. Once the cash draw down is completed, the bank stamps the check as cancelled. Once a check is cancelled, it can no longer be used as an authorization to remove additional funds from the account of the payer. A cancelled check has passed through the entire set of payment activities, which include the following:

1. Received by the payee
2. Endorsed by the payee
3. Deposited with the payee's bank
4. Paid by the drawee bank to the payee bank
5. Cash is paid into the payee's account by the payee bank

A payer can verify whether the checks it has issued have been classified as cancelled by accessing the on-line check record posted by the payer's bank. This information is most commonly used as part of the bank reconciliation process, but can also be used to prove to a payee that a check payment was made, and that the check was cashed.

Less commonly, the bank instead mails all cancelled checks back to the payer along with the monthly bank statement. If so, the payer typically stores the checks as evidence of payment, and eventually shreds them once the company-mandated retention period has passed. A variation on the concept is for the bank to print check images in reduced size on the back of the bank statement, or on accompanying pages.

Deposits in Transit

A deposit in transit is cash and checks that have been received and recorded by an entity, but which have not yet been recorded in the records of the bank where the funds are deposited. If this occurs at month-end, the deposit will not appear in the bank statement issued by the bank, and so becomes a reconciling item in the bank reconciliation prepared by the entity.

A deposit in transit occurs when a deposit arrives at the bank too late for it to be recorded that day, or if the entity mails the deposit to the bank (in which case a mail float of several days can cause an additional delay), or the entity has not yet sent the deposit to the bank at all.

When a company uses a bank lockbox, payments go from customers straight to the bank, at which point the bank records the deposits and then notifies the company of the receipts. In this case, there is no deposit in transit, since the bank's records are updated in advance of the records maintained by the company. If the company is dilatory in recording these deposits, there could even be a reverse deposit in transit, where the bank records the information well before the company.

EXAMPLE

On April 30, Grouch Electronics receives a check from a customer in the amount of $25,000. It records the check as a cash receipt on the same day, and deposits the check at its bank at the end of the day. The bank does not record the check in its books until the following day, May 1. Thus, when Grouch's accountant completes the month-end bank reconciliation, she should add $25,000 to the cash balance shown on the bank statement in order to have it match the cash balance shown in Grouch's accounting records.

Memo Debits

A memo debit is a pending reduction in the cash balance of a bank account, which is a debit transaction. The bank has not yet completely processed the transaction; once it has done so (typically during end-of-day processing), the memo debit designation is replaced by a regular debit transaction, and the cash balance in the bank account is reduced by the amount of the debit.

A memo debit could be a pending outgoing electronic payment, a debit card transaction, a fee to issue new checks, an interest payment on a loan, or a not sufficient funds fee.

Not Sufficient Funds

Earlier, we noted how to deal with not sufficient funds checks. What are they? The not sufficient funds (NSF) designation is a condition where a bank does not honor a check, because the checking account on which it was drawn does not contain sufficient funds.

For example, Mr. Jones writes a check to Mr. Smith for $500, which Mr. Smith deposits. Upon presentation of the check, Mr. Jones' bank refuses to honor it on the grounds that there is only $300 in his checking account. This is a not sufficient funds check.

The recipient of an NSF check (sometimes referred to as a rubber check) may be charged a processing fee by the bank at which it deposited the check. The entity that issues an NSF check is always charged a significant fee by the bank where its checking account is located. Alternatively, if a bank has an overdraft agreement[1] with the party that writes an NSF check, then the bank can instead elect to honor the check and then charge the payer an overdraft fee. In this latter case, the payee's bank accepts the check, so it does not appear on the payee's bank reconciliation as a reconciling item.

A not sufficient funds check is a reconciling item on a bank reconciliation, since if you deposit a check, you assume that it has cleared the bank, whereas a not sufficient funds check has not cleared the bank, thereby reducing the on-hand cash balance.

Outstanding Checks

An outstanding check is a check payment that has been recorded by the issuing entity, but which has not yet cleared its bank account as a deduction from its cash balance. The concept is used in the derivation of the month-end bank reconciliation.

There is typically a multi-day period between when a check is created and when it is presented for payment, which is caused by the time required for the postal service to deliver the check, as well as for the payee to deposit it. The check may also be delayed if the issuing entity puts off mailing the check for any reason.

If an outstanding check has not yet cleared the bank by the end of the month, it does not appear on the month-end bank statement, and so is a reconciling item in the month-end bank reconciliation prepared by the issuing entity.

An outstanding check remains a liability of the payer until such time as the payee presents the check for payment, which then eliminates the liability. If the payee never presents the check for payment, the payer can mark the check as void in its accounting system, which usually marks the original account payable as unpaid, and also increases the balance in the cash account by the amount of the outstanding check that is now being voided.

A common problem for the payer is keeping sufficient cash in a bank account to pay off all outstanding checks, since a few residual checks may not be cashed for a long time (as may be the case with, for example, a rent deposit check or a bid bond). If the payer assumes that an outstanding check will not be cashed and therefore

---

[1] In an overdraft arrangement, a bank charges a fee for accepting a check when the underlying account does not have sufficient funds in it.

reduces the cash balance in the related checking account, this puts the payer at risk of having the check rejected whenever it is finally presented for payment, due to a lack of funds.

Outstanding Deposits

An outstanding deposit (also known as a deposit in transit) is that amount of cash recorded by the receiving entity, but which has not yet been recorded by its bank. All outstanding deposits are listed as reconciling items on the periodic bank reconciliation prepared by the receiving entity. These deposits are subtracted from the book balance of the receiving entity to arrive at the bank balance. Deposits are typically only outstanding for one business day, so there tend to be few of these deposits listed as reconciling items whenever a bank reconciliation is prepared.

For example, a company receives $1,000 on March 31, a Friday, and records it as having been received in March. The bank will record the receipt in the company's account the following Monday, April 3. The $1,000 is considered by the company to be an outstanding deposit until it is recorded by the bank on April 3.

Post-Dated Checks

A post-dated check is a check on which the issuer has stated a date later than the current date. It is used when the issuer wants to delay payment to the recipient, while the recipient may accept it simply because the check represents a firm date on which it will be able to deposit the check. This approach is most commonly used when the payee requires the issuer to hand over a set of post-dated checks to cover a series of future payments, which the payee agrees to cash on the specified dates. This approach is used to improve the odds of being paid, especially when the issuer has little credit.

From the perspective of the issuer, there should be no journal entry to record the reduction in cash until the date listed on the check. From the perspective of the payee, there should be no entry to record the increase in cash until the date listed on the check. Thus, the check date effectively postpones the underlying accounting transaction.

EXAMPLE

Mulligan Imports receives a $500 check payment from a customer for an unpaid invoice on April 30. The check is post-dated to May 15. Mulligan should not record the cash receipt until May 15, nor should it present the check to its bank until that date.

Realistically, the payee may never notice that a check has been post-dated, and so will record and deposit it at once. The bank is also unlikely to notice the date on the check, and in any case may have a policy of honoring all checks at once, irrespective of the check date. In this situation, the check is considered a negotiable instrument, irrespective of the check date, and it is likely that the payee will receive cash from the bank prior to the date on the check. If so, the check will appear on the monthly bank statement.

Returned Checks

A returned check is a check that is not paid by the financial institution on which it was drawn. The usual reason for a returned check is that the account on which it was drawn does not contain enough funds to pay for the full amount of the check (which classifies it as an NSF check). However, the concept of a returned check is somewhat broader than an NSF check, because it might not be paid for the following additional reasons:

- The check is drawn on a foreign account
- The check has been disfigured
- The check contains a mismatch between the numeric and written amount to be paid
- The check was presented for payment too long after the check date
- The check maker issued a stop payment order that blocks payment on the check
- The checking account on which the check was drawn has been closed

Returned Deposits

A returned deposit arises when a company deposits a check with its bank, and the bank refuses to deposit the related amount of cash in the company's bank account. This can happen for the following reasons:

- The bank on which the check was originally drawn rejects the check. This happens when the account on which the check was drawn contains less unencumbered cash than the amount stated on the check.
- There is an error on the check, such as a missing signature, date, payee name, or amount.
- The check was drawn on a bank located in another country, which usually results in an automatic rejection.

Whenever a deposit is returned, the bank does not include it as a source of cash on the month-end bank statement that it sends to the company. If the company had already recorded the deposit in the cash account in its own records, it must reverse this deposit. Otherwise, the book balance of cash will be higher than the bank balance of cash, with the difference being the amount of the returned deposit.

The reversal of the deposit is typically handled through the cash receipts module of the company's accounting software, which will credit the cash account and debit the accounts receivable account (assuming the related check payments were for outstanding invoices due from customers).

In addition, the bank will probably charge a service fee related to the returned deposit, though this amount may be rolled into the total service fee for the month. The company must record the fee as a credit to the cash account and a debit to an expense account.

Uncleared Checks

An uncleared check is a check that has not yet been paid by the bank on which it was drawn. Such a check has already been recorded by the payee and presented to its bank. There is a clearing cycle that must then be completed that lasts several days. During the clearing cycle, the payee's bank presents the check to the payer's bank, which then forwards the cash amount stated on the check to the payee's bank. During the clearing cycle, the payee does not have use of the cash.

Uncollected Funds

Uncollected funds are checks deposited with the payee's bank that have not yet been paid by the bank on which the checks were drawn. The payee's bank must ensure that the funds have been received before it can release them to the payee. In the meantime, the cash is unavailable for use until the funds have been collected by the payee's bank. However, even if these funds are not currently available for use, the associated check will still be listed on the monthly bank statement provided by the bank.

Undeposited Checks

Undeposited checks are checks that have been received from customers and other parties, but not yet deposited. There are several possible reasons why a business might have undeposited checks, including the following:

- The business operates on the cash basis of accounting, and does not want to record any additional income in the current reporting period, in order to avoid reporting additional income.
- The amount of cash represented by the undeposited checks is so small that the accounting manager does not bother to make a deposit, preferring to instead wait for more checks to arrive.
- The checks are post-dated, so the entity cannot yet deposit them.

Ideally, undeposited checks should be reported by the recipient in its balance sheet as cash.

Unpresented Checks

An unpresented check is a check that a payer has created, but which the bank on which the check is drawn has not yet made a corresponding payment to the check recipient (the payee). This may be because the payer has not yet issued the check to the payee, or because the payee has not yet presented the check to the bank for payment.

When constructing a bank reconciliation, you would deduct any unpresented checks from the cash balance calculated by the bank, since the bank does not yet have a record of the check. Thus, if the bank of Curmudgeons International has a balance in its checking account for Curmudgeon of $1,000, and there are $500 of unpresented checks, you would deduct $500 from the $10,000 bank balance to arrive at an adjusted bank balance of $9,500.

When a company issues a check, it is recorded as a credit to the cash account upon issuance (which reduces the balance in the cash account). You would not delay this entry just because it is an unpresented check at that point in time. There are no further journal entries to record in regard to the check, irrespective of whether it has been presented to the bank.

Voided Checks

A voided check is a check that has been cancelled. Once it has been appropriately voided (such as by being perforated with a "Void" stamp), a check cannot be used. There are several possible reasons for a voided check, such as a mistake in filling out the check, or the check was blank and only partially filled in, or the check was issued in error. In all of these cases, the voided check is not used, and so should never appear on a bank reconciliation. However, if a check was issued and then voided, then you must contact the bank and authorize a stop payment on the check (for which the bank will charge a fee). Doing so will block the bank from honoring the check when the payee presents it. This situation may arise when you issue a check for the wrong amount, send it to the wrong party, or realize after the fact that you do not have suffi-cient cash in your checking account to fund the check when it is presented for pay-ment.

In the accounting system, the check would have been recorded when it was orig-inally created, so a reversing entry must be made that debits (increases) cash and cred-its (decreases) the account to which the payment applies. Thus, if the payment had been for an expense, the credit would be to the related expense account; if the payment had been to acquire an asset, the credit would be to the related asset account.

In a computerized accounting system, there is usually a menu option for voiding a check, since this is a sufficiently common activity to warrant having its own routine.

The Daily Bank Reconciliation

The procedure for the monthly bank reconciliation that was just outlined is the stand-ard approach – in terms of its timing. An alternative is to conduct a *daily* bank recon-ciliation, which is based on the daily transactions posted by a bank on its website. By completing a daily reconciliation, it is possible to immediately identify unrecorded incoming cash. In addition, any unusual or unauthorized transactions impacting a cash account can be investigated at once. For example, if a third party fraudulently removes cash from an account with an ACH debit, the accountant can immediately institute a debit block to keep any additional debits from impacting the remaining cash.

The procedure to be followed for a daily bank reconciliation is essentially the same as the one just noted for a monthly reconciliation. We recommend completing it at the beginning of each work day, which makes it easier to contact the bank to discuss and take corrective action regarding any anomalies found. Also, completing this chore early makes it easier to reliably check off the department work list, before other issues take up the remaining time available.

> **Note:** When a company completes a daily bank reconciliation, the bank balance is the ending cash balance appearing on the bank's website for the relevant bank account as of the end of the preceding day.

> **Tip:** Completing a daily bank reconciliation makes it easier to close the books and issue reliable financial statements, since there are unlikely to be many reconciling items left to investigate by the end of the month.

The Proof of Cash

A proof of cash is essentially a roll forward of each line item in a bank reconciliation from one accounting period to the next, incorporating separate columns for cash receipts and cash disbursements. It is more complicated than a bank reconciliation. However, it provides a greater degree of detail, and so makes it easier to locate errors than a bank reconciliation. Thus, it may be cost-effective to use a proof of cash when you expect to find a large number of different cash-related errors within an accounting period.

The columns (and formula) used for a proof of cash are:

Beginning balance + Cash receipts in the period - Cash disbursements in the period
= Ending balance

When used for each line item in a bank reconciliation, the proof of cash highlights areas in which there are discrepancies, and which may therefore require further investigation, and probably some adjusting entries. Examples of these discrepancies are:

- Bank fees not recorded
- NSF checks not deleted from the deposit records
- Interest income or expense not recorded
- Checks or deposits recorded by the bank in different amounts than what they were recorded by the company
- Checks cashed that the company voided
- Cash disbursements and/or receipts recorded in the wrong account

A proof of cash can also uncover instances of fraud. If there is a difference between the totals, it can indicate the presence of unauthorized borrowings and repayments within the time period covered by a single bank statement. For example, if an employee were to illegally withdraw $10,000 from the company accounts near the beginning of the month for his personal use and replace the funds before the end of the month, the issue would not appear in a normal bank reconciliation as a reconciling item. However, a proof of cash would be more likely to flag the extra cash withdrawal and cash return within the period.

Bank Reconciliation Controls

The bank reconciliation itself is an essential control over cash, since it is used not only to verify the cash balance, but also to detect additional expenses. To ensure that this control is effective, make sure that the person responsible for it has no other responsibilities pertaining to cash. If this mandate is not followed, then someone could embezzle cash from the business and then hide this activity by altering the outcome of the bank reconciliation.

Summary

The bank reconciliation is an essential accounting tool, especially for cash accounts that experience a large amount of activity. The possibility of an error in these accounts is so significant that a bank reconciliation should be considered a mandatory part of the month-end closing process. Even for cash accounts with relatively low activity, a reconciliation should be conducted no less frequently than once a quarter. This focus on reconciliations will ensure that the accountant will not be caught with inaccurate cash balances when the auditors examine the books at year-end.

Glossary

B

Bank charge. A fee assessed against an account by a financial institution.

Bank debit. A transaction that reduces the balance in a customer's account at a bank.

Bank error. A transaction that has been incorrectly recorded by a bank in a customer's account.

Bank reconciliation. A comparison of a bank's account balances with an organization's internal financial records.

Bank statement. A document that is issued by a bank once a month to its clients, listing the transactions impacting a bank account.

C

Cancelled check. A check payment for which the stated amount of cash has been removed from the payer's checking account.

D

Deposits in transit. Cash and checks that have been received and recorded by an entity, but which have not yet been recorded in the records of the bank where the funds are deposited.

M

Memo debit. A pending reduction in the cash balance of a bank account, which is a debit transaction.

N

Not sufficient funds. A condition where a bank does not honor a check, because the checking account on which it was drawn does not contain sufficient funds.

O

Outstanding check. A check payment that has been recorded by the issuing entity, but which has not yet cleared its bank account as a deduction from its cash balance.

Outstanding deposit. That amount of cash recorded by the receiving entity, but which has not yet been recorded by its bank.

P

Post-dated check. A check on which the issuer has stated a date later than the current date.

Proof of cash. A roll forward of each line item in a bank reconciliation from one accounting period to the next, incorporating separate columns for cash receipts and cash disbursements.

R

Returned check. A check that is not paid by the financial institution on which it was drawn.

Returned deposit. When a company deposits a check with its bank, and the bank refuses to deposit the related amount of cash in the company's bank account.

U

Uncleared check. A check that has not yet been paid by the bank on which it was drawn.

Uncollected funds. Checks deposited with the payee's bank that have not yet been paid by the bank on which the checks were drawn.

Undeposited checks. Checks that have been received from customers and other parties, but not yet deposited.

Unpresented check. A check that a payer has created, but which the bank on which the check is drawn has not yet made a corresponding payment to the check recipient.

Voided check. A check that has been cancelled.

Index